The Sussex Year

British Library Cataloguing-in-Publication Data.
A catalogue record for this book is available from the British Library.

ISBN 978-0-9559006-5-5

Published by Pomegranate Press, 51 St Nicholas Lane, Lewes, Sussex BN7 2JZ
telephone: 01273 470100; email: sussexbooks@aol.com
website: www.pomegranate-press.co.uk

Printed and bound in China

The Sussex Year

A Country Calendar

David Lang

Above: Floods at Barcombe Mills.

Facing page: Common Tern.

Introduction

I have a clear childhood memory of a radio programme called Children's Hour on what was then, in the early 1940s, the BBC Home Service. At that time there was a regular feature by a broadcaster with the pseudonym Romany, who described the birds, animals and flowers he had seen at that time of year on walks in the countryside.

Later he published a book, *Through the Years with Romany*, which was a favourite of mine and probably laid the foundation for a lifetime's interest in natural history.

My career as a country veterinary surgeon in Sussex gave me great opportunities to enjoy the outstanding wealth of plant and bird life in the county, and to photograph what I saw. Some readers may detect a bias towards the wild orchids of Sussex, but I would plead in mitigation that Sussex has one of the richest orchid floras of any county in Great Britain.

This book is an attempt to whet your appetite, and to encourage you to discover for yourself the treasures that await you. Like the Romany book, it takes you through the year from January to December.

David Lang
Barcombe, 2009

January

Faced with bitter cold winds, rain, snow and ice, it is all too easy to stay indoors and shelter from the weather. Yet this is a wonderful time of year to get out into the country to witness the extraordinary variety and numbers of birds which breed north of Great Britain and which overwinter in our more friendly climate.

Sussex may not attract the huge flocks of geese, ducks and swans to be seen on the east coasts of Scotland and England, but it can still boast impressive displays of these winter visitors in its river valleys and wetlands.

Away from the coast, wintering flocks of Redwings and Fieldfares will be demolishing the few berries remaining on holly trees, hawthorn bushes and cotoneaster, while garden birds such as Blue Tits, Great Tits, Greenfinches and the occasional Nuthatch and woodpecker benefit from the food that we put out for them – an increasingly important service in maintaining our wild bird populations.

Above: Oak on the Crink at Barcombe.

Facing page: Wader flocks at Thorney Island. At low tide huge flocks of Godwits, Knot, Dunlin, Sanderling and plovers feed on the mudflats and make a stunning spectacle when they take to the skies after being disturbed by a hunting Peregrine.

Caburn in snow. In most winters the snowfall in Sussex is light, occurring mainly in January and February, but on occasions, such as the winter of 1965–66, heavy snowfall coming in from the Continent across south-east England can bring everything to a standstill. This photograph shows the Caburn on 'the morning after', when I had to drive from Lewes to Firle on an emergency call to a sick cow. Mine was the only vehicle on the road – if you discount the two Sunblest Bakery vans upside down in the ditches.

Bewick's Swans, which breed in Arctic Russia, winter in flocks in a number of river valleys, from Rye Harbour and Pett Level in the east to the Arun Valley in the west. Smaller than the resident Mute Swans, they tend to stand more erect with straight necks, especially if they are apprehensive. Close up you can see their triangular yellow bills with black tips. The much large Whooper Swans also have black and yellow bills, and similarly frequent riverside pastures, but they are less commonly seen in Sussex.

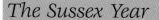

The bird which left its tracks in the snow seems to have made rather a bad landing! It's fascinating to get out in the countryside after an overnight fall of snow, and to read what the birds and animals have been doing by examining the tracks they have left – something which small children really enjoy doing.

Hamsey church, near Lewes, marooned by floods in 1968. Tradition relates that the Witenagemot – a gathering of the 10th century court – was held there on a number of occasions. This was a wise choice, since the mound was surrounded by water and could be reached only by means of a narrow causeway. It was a simple matter to check on all those attending, and to disarm them if necessary.

Malling Down under snow.

Many of our Sussex rivers drain huge catchment areas in the north of the county, flowing south and through the chain of the South Downs, where they are constricted. After very heavy rain the flow becomes too great to be contained by the river banks, and flooding ensues, particularly if the lower reaches of the river are tidal and this coincides with a spring tide and a strong south-westerly wind. The valley of the River Ouse north of Lewes floods with regularity. This view was taken in 2007 near Barcombe Mills.

Hawthorn under snow.

Brent Geese winter in west Sussex in large numbers, particularly in Pagham and Chichester harbours, where they feed on eelgrass exposed at low tide. Small flocks can also be seen in the east at Cuckmere Haven, Pett Level, Pevensey Levels and Rye Harbour.

Ducks on a scrape.

Ashdown Forest in winter.

February

Early February often suffers the most bitterly cold weather of the winter, with snow and heavy rain. Many Redwings and Fieldfares, having eaten all the available berries, move on to the West Country and Ireland, while freezing conditions in Holland and Germany push more ducks, geese and wild swans into southern England. Out on the marshes and brooklands Short-eared Owls and the occasional Hen Harrier hunt for mice and voles, especially as the evening comes on.

Even on the coldest, darkest nights Tawny Owls start calling, as they breed early in the year and are establishing their territories. For the same reason you can often hear foxes barking – the vixens making an eerie scream.

Towards mid-February Rooks and Herons return to their breeding territories and begin the task of building and rebuilding their nests high up in the trees after the damage caused by winter storms.

In the latter part of the month the first early lambs are born within the shelter of the lambing yards.

Above: February probably sees the largest concentration of wintering Wigeon, which graze pasture in the river valleys during the day, roosting out on the sea or on reservoirs for safety at night. The smart males can be distinguished by a prominent white patch on each wing.

Facing page: The Downs near Wolstonbury Hill. Towards the end of the month a few fine days presage the coming spring.

Left: Drake Shoveler. Small groups of Shoveler can be found among the wintering Wigeon. The males are resplendent in black, white and chestnut plumage, with glossy green heads and huge bills. They prefer to stay on water, frequenting lakes, dykes and gravel pits.

Below: February woods in snow.

Above: The first primroses can be found in flower on sheltered sunny banks protected from the cold winds.

Right: Waxwings at Seaford. Waxwings winter south of their breeding territories in north and north-east Europe, and in certain years a shortage of food sees large numbers crossing the North Sea westwards to Great Britain in 'Waxwing eruptions'. Most of the flocks stay on the east coast, but a few make their way to Sussex, appearing in gardens and, particularly, supermarket car parks, which are often planted with berry-bearing shrubs.

Food is in short supply in February, and these beautiful birds are so keen to feed that they almost ignore you. The dark wings, boldly marked white and yellow, have scarlet waxy tips to the secondary wing feathers, which give the bird its common name, while the head is crowned with a pinkish-chestnut crest. A 'Waxwing year' is a memorable event for those fortunate enough to experience it.

March

March has the reputation for wild and unpredictable weather, with south-westerly gales, rain and fine weather alternating with cold and frosts. This is reflected in the flowers and the wildlife we find. The wintering birds are getting restless and ready to depart north, while a few summer visitors are beginning to appear sporadically along the south coast. Birdwatchers at Selsey Bill, Brighton Marina, Seaford and Beachy Head gather to watch the vanguard of the armada of seabirds which migrate each year from the Atlantic and Bay of Biscay up the Channel to the North Sea and finally to their Arctic breeding grounds.

When the conditions are favourable thousands of Gannets, Guillemots, and Razorbills, with Red- and Black-throated Divers and Arctic Skuas, can be seen streaming past – a sight of which most people are totally unaware. This part of early spring is eagerly awaited by enthusiasts.

The first spring flowers are beginning to appear after the drabness of winter, many of them well known and loved, while others less well known, but no less attractive, brighten springtime walks in the countryside.

Facing page: The mass of blossoms of Blackthorn (*Prunus spinosa*) are a glad sight in hedgerows all over Sussex. Their flowering often seems to coincide with a cold snap, known as a 'blackthorn winter' – short lasting, but nonetheless chilly.

Right: Wild Daffodils (*Narcissus pseudonarcissus*) flower in late March, mainly in woodlands and most frequently on the clay soils of the Weald. It is a native plant, but it can be naturalised from introduced stock, although the form is not often found in cultivation. This fine group was in woodland near Plumpton.

A dewpond near Keymer Post in early March reflects something of the bleakness of the weather.

Clockwise from above: Wood Anemones (*see page 25*); Marsh-marigolds (*Altha palustris*) come into flower in mid-March. They are locally common alongside streams, in ditches and on the banks of ponds; Common Dog-violet (*Viola riviniana*), with its heart-shaped leaves and sharply pointed sepals, is common and widespread throughout Sussex in woodland and hedge banks, making a welcome splash of colour; Giant Butter-bur (*Petasites japonicus*) is a rare introduction, found in a few damp hedgerows throughout the county. When it first appears the mound of creamy flowers set in a frame of soft, pale green leaves is most attractive – until it starts to grow up and loses the appearance of a bridal bouquet.

Right: Early Forget-me-not (*Mysotis ramosissima*) is one of the most attractive of the genus, flowering from the end of the month and throughout early summer, mainly on the chalk grassland of the Downs, although it is also found on sandy soils. It is tiny, with bristly, hairy leaves and dense heads of dark blue flowers. Later the stems elongate and the flower heads unfurl, losing their attractive shape.

Bottom right: Mezereon (*Daphne mezereum*) is well known as a garden plant, the leafless stems in March covered with masses of sweetly scented mauve flowers. Wild Mezereon was known in Sussex only from Glynde Holt, where this photograph was taken in 1968, but it has now disappeared, as it has from many of its sites on the chalk in southern England. The wild form has few flowers and produces them at the same time as the leaves, unlike the cultivar. Its demise may be due to overgrowth by more robust shrubs in woods no longer maintained as they were in the past.

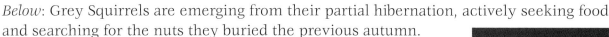

Below: Grey Squirrels are emerging from their partial hibernation, actively seeking food and searching for the nuts they buried the previous autumn.

Wood Anemone (*Anemone nemorosa*) is one of the joys of early spring, growing throughout Sussex in broadleaf woodland, hedgerows and copses. It can carpet the ground with its flowers in recently felled or coppiced woodland, decreasing over the following years as the tree cover increases, only to reappear in profusion when the coppicing is repeated. Look for the very attractive forms with pink or, less commonly, blue-flushed undersides to their petals.

April

April in the Sussex countryside is one of the most delightful times of the year. The first Cuckoos are calling from early April onwards: tradition has it that the Old Lady lets the first one out of a basket at Heffle (Heathfield) Fair on 14th April. Early in the month the first Sand Martins arrive, closely followed by Swallows and House Martins. Spring has properly arrived!

Everywhere the resident songbirds are declaring their territories. Thrushes, Blackbirds and Robins are in full song, while incoming migrants from Africa – Chiffchaffs, Blackcaps and the first Willow Warblers – add to the music. Green and Great-spotted Woodpeckers are drumming in the woodlands, where we can also hear the piping calls of Nuthatches and the trilling of Treecreepers.

Everywhere spring flowers are beginning to appear in good numbers, especially on the Downs where Cowslips flourish. In the past their numbers declined severely as people dug them up to put in their gardens or picked the flowers to make cowslip wine. In the last decade they have recovered spectacularly and we can once again enjoy slopes covered with their flowers.

Above: Great Crested Grebes breed regularly on ponds, lakes and reservoirs across Sussex, laying eggs as early as the end of February in floating nests constructed of reeds and green vegetation. The mating display involves the male bringing beaks full of nesting material to offer to his mate, accompanied by much calling and head-shaking. By April many of the eggs have hatched, and the attractive striped chicks are often seen carried on the back of the adult, partly hidden by the wings.

Facing page: Cowslips on downland chalk in Caburn Bottom, near Lewes.

Early morning can be a lovely time to be on top of the Downs, as here at Blackcap, with the sun clearing the mist from the land below, giving a softness of texture to the view.

April butterflies, clockwise from above: Alongside road verges and woodland rides Brimstones bring a bright assurance that spring really has arrived; the Dingy Skipper (a dreary name for a delightful insect) is often the first butterfly to be seen in spring on warm, sunny chalk banks on the Downs; the diminutive and charming Holly Blue (the upper wing surface dark blue and the underside a stunning silvery blue with tiny black marks) is seen in parks and gardens near its food plants, Holly, Dogwood and Ivy; the Speckled Wood is widely distributed in broadleaf woodland, frequenting sunny hedgerows and sheltered glades. Like the Holly Blue, it has a second brood in August.

Coralroot (*Dentaria bulbifera*) is a rare and very local plant found in woodlands mainly in north-east Sussex near Tunbridge Wells. The flowers are larger and more striking than those of Lady's-smock or Cuckooflower (*C. pratensis*), which is common in wet ditches and roadsides throughout the county. The other distinguishing feature of Coralroot is the purple-brown bulbils in the axils of the upper leaves, by which the plant reproduces.

Ramsons (*Allium ursinum*) are the most common of the twenty wild garlics which occur in Britain. The plant flourishes along the banks of streams in woodland. It is not particularly palatable, and the smell is so strong that it can be detected even in a passing car with the windows shut. Cows can become addicted to it, breaking down fences to get into the woods where it grows. This renders their milk absolutely undrinkable.

Knowlands Wood, near Barcombe. April is bluebell time, one of the great pleasures of spring being a walk through the woods in which they flourish. The native Bluebell (*Hyacinthoides non-scriptus*) is threatened in some woods by the alien Spanish Bluebell (*H. hispanica*), which hybridizes with it, the hybrid then tending to out-compete our native bluebell. Care should be taken never to dump unwanted garden bluebells in the countryside.

Lewes from Kingston Ridge.

Cowslips (*Primula veris*) have made a great recovery on the Downs. (*See also page 24.*)

Avocets, the emblem of the RSPB, are nowadays a regular feature of the spring influx of migrants, particularly in April when small flocks can be seen moving along the coast. As elsewhere in England, they now breed regularly in wetlands at both the west and east ends of the county, and they also winter with us – a graceful addition to the birds of Sussex.

More violet species are now coming into flower, as here near Belle Tout on the coast near Beachy Head, where clearance of gorse and scrub resulted in a spectacular display of Hairy Violet (*Viola hirta*) – well named for its hairy leaves and flower stalks. (*See page 38.*)

Beech leaves in spring.

Kithurst Hill, north-west of Findon.

The Early-purple Orchid (*Orchis mascula*) is usually associated with woodlands but can also be found flowering abundantly on the Downs and above the cliffs at Beachy Head. With their large spikes of mauve flowers and leaves marked with large spots and blotches, they are easy to identify. When the flowers first open they smell sweet, but this rapidly changes after pollination to a stink reminiscent of cats' urine – a signal to would-be insect pollinators not to waste their time. White-flowered plants (*above right*) are not unusual.

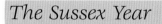

Above: Pasqueflower (*Pulsatilla vulgaris*) has never been proven to occur in Sussex. It is a rare plant of chalk and limestone pastures in southern and eastern England, but there is an old story that it was once found in flower in Bible Bottom on the Downs east of Lewes.

Below: Wild Wallflower (*Erysium cheiri*) is an introduced species, from which the garden cultivars were derived. It grows on chalk, and can be found on the cliffs at Seaford and Beachy Head. Almost invariably yellow-flowered, it has a compact form and a sweet scent.

Hairy Violet.

Above Fulking.

May

May is usually a month of settled, fine weather – a good time to get out into the countryside and enjoy the wealth of flowers and wildlife that Sussex contains. The early flowering orchids are a particular delight on the Downs, and it is interesting to note that in these days when 'global warming' is such an issue they are coming into flower 10–14 days earlier than they did fifty years ago. This is not the case, however, for species flowering later in the year, where the dates remain unaltered.

Everywhere the song birds are now in full voice, and a walk along the river banks where there are good reed beds will be punctuated by the chattering songs of Reed and Sedge Warblers.

Facing page: The Downs at Blackcap. The grass is full of the yellow flowers of Common Rock-rose (*Helianthemum nummularium*), the food plant of the Brown Argus butterfly, which is on the wing for much of May.

Above right: Midland Hawthorn (*Crataegus laevigata*) is easily overlooked, as it closely resembles its more frequent relative, Common Hawthorn. It has shiny leaves with rounded lobes, while the more showy flowers bear two stigmas at the centre, not one as in Common Hawthorn (*C. monogyna*). It is thought to be a relict species of ancient woodland, surviving in hedgerows on clay soils.

Clockwise from right: Early Gentian (*Gentianella anglica*) is a rare flower of chalk grassland, with an erratic and highly sporadic appearance; Common Milkwort (*Polygala vulgaris*) grows on the Downs but is also frequent elsewhere, with flowers of bright blue, intermediate in colour between the other two milkworts; Chalk Milkwort (*Polygala calcarea*) is locally common on the chalk downs of east Sussex. The dwarf habit and pale blue flowers clustered in a tight head distinguish it from the taller, darker blue-flowered Heath Milkwort, which is frequent on acid heaths and grassland, flowering from late May into late summer; Field Fleawort (*Senecio integrifolius*) is confined to short chalk grassland. Unlike its close relative Ragwort (*S. jacobea*), it is a small, neat plant with just a few relatively large flowers on the stem. Many of the places where it grows are Iron Age sites, and it is thought to have been brought to Sussex by early settlers from the area of Sweden, Denmark and North Jutland. The crushed foliage and flowers were put in bedding to discourage fleas.

White Helleborine (*Cephalanthera damasonium*) likes mature beech woods, usually on chalky soils, its distribution chiefly following the line of the South Downs. It is thriving and increasing in Friston Forest. The creamy white flowers scarcely open, but a careful examination of the lip shows it to bear five parallel yellow ridges.

Mousetail (*Myosurus minimus*) is a very rare and intriguing relative of the buttercup. The cylindrical receptacle in the centre of the flowers elongates in fruit to 3–7cm in length, the tail-like structure giving the plant its name. It likes a damp environment: these were growing around a cattle trough in a field near Henfield.

The end of the month often brings surprises, such as this Small Elephant-hawk moth which turned up in my garden.

On downland, grassland and woodland rides throughout Sussex, Common Blue butterflies can be abundant. Here a male feeds on the nectar of thyme.

The Green Hairstreak is most often to be found in scrubby wasteland on hawthorn, where the males sit tilting their wings to reflect the bright green underside and attact a mate. Close examination shows them to be wearing smart white socks!

Small Blue butterflies are widespread but very local, colonies persisting for years in hollows on the Downs or in sheltered chalk pits, the caterpillars feeding on Kidney Vetch.

Despite its name, the Brown Argus is a member of the blue butterfly family. The first brood appears in May, the second in late July – restricted to chalk downland where the caterpillars' major feed plant, Common Rock-rose, grows.

By late May young nestling Swallows are well grown, with voracious appetites to keep their harassed parents busy.

Some May-flowering plants, left to right:

Heath Dog-violet (*Viola canina*) is common on heaths and sandy soils. However, it does occasionally flower near the coast on the chalk, these plants having an attractively constrasting yellow spur, as seen here.

Late May is the flowering time for Sword-leaved Helleborine (*Cephalanthera longifolia*), an elegant relative of White Helleborine and similarly a plant of mature beech woods. It is decreasing throughout its range, and in Sussex is now known only in a few sites in the extreme west.

Green-winged Orchid (*Orchis morio*), traditionally a flower of damp meadows, also occurs on lawns, in cemeteries and even on roundabouts in the middle of main roads. In appearance similar to the Early-purple Orchid, this species has unspotted leaves, and the outer sepals of the hood of the flower are strongly marked with parallel green veins. White- and pink-flowered forms are recorded.

Burnt Orchid (*Orchis ustulata*) comes into flower about the third week in May. This tiny but charming orchid is nationally rare and threatened, being restricted to ancient chalk grassland, where it favours steep slopes terraced by the feet of passing sheep. It takes about 16 years to reach flowering maturity from seed and cannot tolerate competition from coarse vegetation such as tor grass, which has spread so much in recent years. It has disappeared from much of its range in Sussex and elsewhere, but still maintains one large population near Lewes. There is another form which flowers later in the year. *(See page 70.)*

Marsh-orchids have had a hard time in the last fifty years, as marshes and damp pastures have been drained. Early Marsh-orchid (*Dactylorhiza incarnata*) can still be found in a few scattered sites . Subspecies *incarnata* (*right*) has pale pink flowers attractively marked with red loops and spots. Ssp *pulchella* has mauve-coloured flowers and is more often found on wet, acid heaths, such as Ashdown Forest.

Early Spider Orchid (*Ophrys sphegodes*) was first recorded in Sussex in 1834 near Birling Gap, and still remains in a number of sites in that area, but the largest population is in Castle Hill National Nature Reserve. The flowers resemble large, furry spiders and are pollinated by male Solitary Bees (*top right*), which mistake the flower for a female bee. A

rare colour form of this orchid (*above*) has been recorded several times in Sussex. The flowers of var.*lutea* lack the usual brown pigments, resulting in startling flowers of yellow and white.

The Seven Sisters from the mouth of the Cuckmere River.

June

T he long daylight hours and usually fine weather make June a most attractive month. Everywhere birds are hard at work foraging on behalf of their nestlings, and whether you visit the woods, the open Downs, the marshes or the coastal cliffs and shingles, there is always something interesting to see.

On a fine warm evening, as dusk falls, there is a good chance of hearing a Nightingale in full song in woodland, or in places such as the scrub along the sides of abandoned railway lines, some of which have become public footpaths.

Evening is also the time to visit the healthlands of west Sussex or Ashdown Forest in the east to listen for the churring song of the Nightjar. Sit quietly and wait, but be prepared for attack by midges.

The following photographs can only show a fraction of the riches to be found, but they should whet your appetite to see more.

Facing page: Viper's-bugloss (*Echium vulgare*) is a common plant of light, dry soils, often by the sea and on the Downs, as here in Malling Coombe above Lewes. The tall spikes of flowers are very bristly and usually of a sky-blue colour, but white and also pink flowers can frequently be found. They are rich in nectar, attracting many bees and butterflies.

Above right: The Man Orchid (*Aceras anthropophorum*) is well named, for the little flowers, greenish-yellow or russet brown, have a lip divided into four lobes like two arms and two legs. It grew on the edge of a field at Alciston until 1966, when it was destroyed by spraying. Another good colony on the Crumbles west of Pevensey was destroyed when the marina was constructed in 1969. Always rare in Sussex, it is now only to be found at Wolstonbury Hill.

One of the strangest plants to be found near Beachy Head is the tiny annual Small Hare's-ear (*Bupleurum baldense*). It is a member of the larger Umbellifer family, which includes carrots, parsnips and fennel, but this flower is only to be found elsewhere in Britain in a single location in south Devon. The minute yellow flowers are fringed by a cup of pointed bracteoles. It grows on the very edge of the cliffs where the turf is crumbling away into the void, which makes close-up photography a trifle nerve-wracking.

Sea-kale (*Crambe maritima*) grows on shingle beaches all along the south coast, and is pictured here at the Crumbles, near Eastbourne. The leaves (purple tinged when they first uncurl) are just about edible but should not be picked.

Biting Stonecrop (*Sedum acre*) is a common plant near the sea. In 1988 ground at Tide Mills near Newhaven was levelled for projected railway sidings, to be promptly covered with a spectacular showing of this yellow stonecrop.

Ten species of Broomrapes are found in Britain, of which four still flower in Sussex. They have no leaves or green chlorophyll, being parasitic on the roots of other plants. Their common names relate to their host plant. Knapweed Broomrape (*Orobanche elatior*) is a magnificent and rare species, parasitic on Greater Knapweed (*Centaurea scabiosa*), which is itself a common plant on the Sussex Downs.

Left: Meadow Crane's-bill (*Geranium pratense*) is often grown in gardens, so that many of the plants we see are probably not native. In recent years its welcome splash of colour has become more common on road verges in the county.

Right and below: Common Spotted-orchids (*Dactylorhiza fuchsii*) flower throughout June and July in a wide variety of habitats. The main picture shows a mass of flowers on a road verge just outside Arundel. Colour variation is considerable.

Wall Brown butterflies have two broods, the first emerging in mid-May, the second in late July. They enjoy basking in sunny country lanes and in sheltered field corners.

Pearl-bordered Fritillaries are on the wing from late May and throughout June. The caterpillars feed on the leaves of Dog Violet and Heartsease, which are to be found in sunny rides and clearings in broadleaf woodland. Sadly this butterfly has become very scarce in recent years.

The Painted Lady butterfly is a migrant from Africa which crosses the Mediterranean and Europe to reach us. In some years swarms of them arrive in early summer, flying in low over the water. Often found in gardens, the butterfly is particularly fond of the flowers of wild thistles.

Shelducks nest in burrows in grassland and sand-dunes. This family was pictured on the Cuckmere at Exceat.

Firle Beacon from the Caburn.

Right: It's a red letter day when you see a Hoopoe in Sussex. After wintering south of the Mediterranean, they migrate north to Europe in the spring. A few overshoot, crossing the Channel and turning up along the Sussex coast and occasionally inland, as here at Wych Cross. Hoopoes have been known to breed in Sussex, and with climate change this may happen again.

Fragrant orchids (*Gymnadenia conopsea*) are most commonly to be found on the grassy sides of the Downs, and three sub-species grow in Sussex. The common form, ssp.*conopsea (left),* grows mainly on the Downs from the west of Sussex to Beachy Head. The lip of the flower is divided into three well developed, rounded lobes, the central one much longer than the others, while the sepals droop downwards.

Ssp.*densiflora* (right) is a much larger plant, growing in a few places on north-facing slopes of the Downs where moisture seepage lines come to the surface.

The third form, ssp.*borealis* (*far right*) flowers later, usually on acid soils.

Above and detail top: Two species of Butterfly-orchid occur in Sussex, of which Greater Butterfly-orchid (*Platanthera chlorantha*) is the more frequent, particularly in West Sussex woods. It likes to grow in light, dappled shade. The long nectar-filled spur at the back of each flower attracts night-flying moths such as the Silver-Y and Elephant Hawk-moth.

Far right and detail: The Fly Orchid (*Ophrys insectifera*) enjoys dappled shade, especially under trees in beech woods, but in recent years it has disappeared from many of its known sites. The flowers are amazingly like insects in shape. Pollination is effected by male Digger Wasps, which are fooled by the scent and attempt to mate with the flower.

Downland near High and Over, Alfriston.

Left: The curious looking Bird's-nest Orchid (*Neottia nidus-avis*) is found in beech woods across Sussex. Devoid of leaves and chlorophyll, it is a honey-brown colour, usually growing close to beech trees on which it is partly dependent as a hemi-parasite. The name derives from the tangled mass of fleshy roots, which resemble a badly made bird's nest.

Centre: Heath Spotted-orchid (*Dactylorhiza maculata* ssp.*ericetorum*) grows in old meadows on clay or acid soils, and particularly on heathland, such as the heaths of west Sussex and Ashdown Forest. It flowers some two weeks later than the Common Spotted-orchid and has similarly spotted leaves.

Right: Common Marsh-orchid (*Dactylorhiza praetermissa*) comes into flower at the end of the month. Tall and robust, it is widely distributed across Sussex in damp meadows and marshes, but is never common.

The Bee Orchid (*Ophrys apifera*) (*above and inset*) is the best known of all our native orchids. Mainly associated with chalk downland, it also thrives on road verges, especially those recently built. Although the flowers closely resemble bees, they are almost exclusively self-pollinated. In a number of places along the Sussex coast flowers with white sepals and a greenish tip (var.*cholorantha*) occur (*bottom left*). The abnormal form (*top right*), where the 'bee' has been replaced by a structure like a pink sepal, has only ever been found in Sussex, last appearing in 1972. The variety *atrofuscus* (*bottom right*) is also entirely restricted to Sussex. It was found near Warnham in 2001 and again in 2006.

Jack and Jill windmills, seen from Wolstonbury Hill – the only place in Sussex (*see page 51*) to find Man Orchids.

Roses of many species can be found in flower in Sussex – some rare and others, like the Dog Rose, to be found nearly everywhere. Burnet Rose (*Rosa pimpinellifolia*), pictured here at The Caburn, is locally frequent on chalky soils. The hips which form in autumn are unique among English roses, being blackish-purple.

July

Although the weather of July is so often unreliable, there are still plenty of flowers and butterflies to be enjoyed. Many birds have stopped singing, their young already fledged and flown the nest, so there is no need for them to defend a territory. Despite that, harassed adults can often be encountered being pestered by importuning youngsters which are fatter and fluffier than their parents.

Some butterfly species that first emerged earlier in the summer have a second brood towards the end of the month, such as Wall Brown, Hedge Brown, Small Tortoiseshell and Peacock. In a few favoured woods the superb Purple Emperor can still be seen, especially on a warm afternoon when they will descend from their perches high up in the tree canopy.

July may not be the most prolific month for exciting wild flowers, but it still has a great deal to offer us before it is time to enjoy the colours and fruits of the autumn.

Above: Dyer's Greenweed (*Genista tinctoria*) makes a welcome splash of colour in rough grasslands, most often on clay soils. Recently is appears to be on the increase, particularly on the Downs. In times past extracts of the plant were used as a yellow dye.

Facing page: The South Downs, looking west from Newtimber Hill.

Above: July is the time to look for Wild Strawberry (*Fragaria vesca*), which is not uncommon in sheltered hedgerows and woodland rides on chalky and basic soils. The fruits are not as large as those of cultivated strawberries, but what they lack in size they make up for in flavour. The first reference to them is in a Saxon plant list of the 10th century, and 'straberie' are mentioned in the household roll of the Countess of Leicester in 1265.

Left: This month is also a fine time for flowering thistles, the finest being Musk Thistle (*Carduus nutans*). It is common in rough ground on chalky soils, where the big, nodding purple heads attract scores of butterflies.

July butterflies, clockwise from above: First brood Comma butterflies emerge during the month. The underside of the wings is dusky brown, the rear wings marked with a white comma, giving the butterfly its name. It is common in gardens and parks, as well as the countryside; a Meadow Brown nectaring on Common Knapweed, an important source of energy for many butterflies in high summer. The undersides of the wings, with their prominent 'eyes', are more attractive than the upper sides; the Marbled White, a common sight in rough downland grass, in woodland and on road verges, is often seen alongside the Meadow Brown, and this photographs shows a female also feeding on Common Knapweed; the Silver-washed Fritillary is a large and beautiful butterfly of woodlands, where the caterpillars feed on the leaves of Sweet Violet. The upper wing surface is a rich foxy brown, the underside marked with a silver and green wave pattern. The best time to see them is late afternoon, when they descend to nectar on bramble blossom. Their flight is strong, the males chasing the females and rival males at high speed along sunny rides in the woods.

Above: Spiked Rampion (*Phyteuma spicatum*) is a nationally rare flower, confined to east Sussex, with several roadside colonies near Heathfield and a single wood near Hailsham. The tall, graceful spikes of creamy yellow flowers appear from late June throughout July.

Left: Caburn from Itford ridge.

Above: Yellow Bird's-nest (*Monotropa hypopitys*) is a strange plant of beech woods, where there is a deep accumulation of rotted leaves. It is a saprophyte, like the Bird's-nest Orchid, but the drooping yellow flowers are distinctive.It flowered prolifically in Friston Forest in 2008.

Right: Until the 1930s the Lizard Orchid (*Himantoglossum hircinum*) was recorded all across southern England, including many sites in Sussex. In 1919 a schoolgirl collecting wild flowers for a flower show at Plumpton picked one, thinking it was a Butterfly-orchid. When it opened she realised it was not and sent it to the British Museum, where it is still preserved in the herbarium. In the early 1940s the country suffered a series of bitterly cold winters, and the plants disappeared, except for a few at Camber and in Kent, near Sandwich. Recently there has been a resurgence of populations in southern England, and in Sussex they have reappeared in some of their classic locations. As they are common roadside plants in northern France, windblown seed may account for new records on the south coast, while a milder climate may see them spread once more. The flowers have a very strange shape, looking as if a lizard has dived inside, leaving its hind legs and long tail protruding. The scent is very strong, resembling that of a billy goat.

Left: Burnt Orchid is traditionally considered as flowering in May in Sussex, but records made since 1965 show that we have a late-flowering form, provisionally named *Orchis ustulata* ssp.*serotina*. The flowers appear in late July and August and are much more darkly pigmented than the early form. The flower hood does not fade, but remains dark red, and the spots on the lip are big and dark red also. Some flowers may have the entire lip flushed red. It is known in 16 sites between Lewes and Eastbourne, with two sites recorded in Hampshire and four in Wiltshire but nowhere else, making it something of a Sussex speciality. This late form was not recognised until recently, although old records go back as far as July 1849 near Eastbourne.

Right: Pyramidal Orchid (*Anacamptis pyramidalis*) is mainly to be found on chalk soils, but large populations also occur on coastal golf links at Littlehampton, Shoreham, Rye and Camber. Small populations are also to be found on the heaths of west Sussex and on road verges away from the Downs. It is highly successful at colonising new ground, such as the sides of motorways and roundabouts. It spreads from seed, and the number flowering can vary greatly from year to year.

Above: The little Musk Orchid (*Herminium monorchis*) is entirely restricted to very short turf on the South Downs. It was literally burned up by the severe drought in the summer of 1976 and is now scarce.

Left: Firle Beacon from Windover Hill.

Above and detail: July is the time to look for Frog Orchids (*Coeloglossum viride*). They occur on the chalk from west Sussex to Beachy Head in the east, favouring short downland turf. They are often found by prehistoric barrows, at ancient chalk workings, and around the edges of dewponds, where they can be abundant. The flowers can be yellow-green or a mixture of green and brown, and they are not easy to spot. They have the honour of being the first orchid in Sussex to be described in print, named by C. Merrett in 1666 as *Orchis batrachoides autumnalis flore luteo*, growing near Lewes. It is not clear whether C. Merrett is the same person as Christopher Merret of Lewes who invented the champagne process in 1672 – something the French tend to ignore.

The Bog Orchid (*Hammarbya paludosa*) was always a scarce plant in Sussex, restricted to sphagnum moss bogs – a habitat which has slowly disappeared as the result of drainage and afforestation. The last plants were known near Wych Cross in the 1950s, but there is always the hope that they may live on.

Probably one of our best known butterflies, the Small Tortoiseshell is a great feature of late summer, especially in gardens where there are Buddleja bushes in flower. The first brood appears at the very end of June, flourishing in July, with a second brood in late August which can still be on the wing in late October. The caterpillars feed on Stinging Nettles, which is a good excuse for leaving a bit of garden uncultivated. Many of the late brood will overwinter in garden sheds and even in houses.

The White Admiral butterfly is one of the most beautiful to be seen in Sussex. They breed on Honeysuckle in broadleaf woodland, emerging in early July, and are on the wing into August. Like the Silver-washed Fritillaries, they tend to stay high up in the tree canopy, coming down to feed on bramble blossom on sunny afternoons.

The earliest of the autumn-flowering helleborines to flower is Pendulous-flowered Helleborine (*Epipactis phyllanthes*). It was first described in 1852 by G.E. Smith in an article in the *Gardener's Chronicle*, the specific name being said to derive from Phillis Wood near Treyford in west Sussex. It is now rare and under threat, growing in a few places on shaded road verges, mainly in west Sussex, where it suffers from the passing traffic and ill-considered roadworks. It is also attractive to Roedeer, which eat the flower spikes. One distinguishing feature is the fat, pear-shaped ovary.

Above: Green beetle on *Hieracium*.

Right: Spurge-laurel (*Daphne laureola*) is relatively common in beech woods on the chalk and in hedgerows on basic soils. It is very easily overlooked, being a small evergreen shrub with dense clusters of yellow-green flowers hiding under the shiny leaves. In late July the juicy black berries ripen, but disappear remarkably quickly from the plants, probably taken by bank voles or woodmice, who leave neat little piles of berry skins and the opened stones from which the seeds have been removed. The fruits are poisonous, containing a visicant resin mezerine, which blisters the mouth and tongue, followed by dysentery and collapse. However, they taste so foul that cases of poisoning among children and farm animals are rare.

August

Despite the warm summer days, there is already a hint that autumn is just around the corner. Migrant birds which have finished rearing their young are showing signs of restlessness. By mid-August the 'screaming parties' of Swifts will have departed south, while Swallows and House Martins are starting to gather on the telephone wires, the young Swallows easy to spot by the lack of the long outer tail feathers of their parents.

Hobbys may appear overhead and dash in to snatch the young and unwary House Martins. The first autumn migrants appear, especially along the coast, among them wading birds which have bred in the Arctic, and unusual vagrant warblers and flycatchers which have been blown off course on their journey from the north to Africa.

The month of August is excellent for unusual flowers, both on the Downs and in the woods, but best of all this is the start of the autumn fruit season, with the first ripe berries appearing on wayside bushes, while the sound of the combine harvester is heard in the land.

Poppies are a feature of the edges of cornfields, as at Race Hill (*left*) on the outskirts of Lewes. Common Poppies (*Papaver rhoeas*) make a bold splash of colour, with (*right*) the occasional white flower among them.

Two interesting flowers which occur on the coastal shingles are Broad-leaved Everlasting-pea (*Lathyrus latifolia*) (*left*) and Common Dodder (*Cuscuta epithymum*), the latter parasitic on Dwarf Broom. Both species can be found elsewhere on rough grassy areas, the Everlasting-pea occurring with increasing frequency near railway lines and the Dodder as a parasite on Heather.

Common Terns nest regularly in three colonies in Sussex – at Rye Harbour in the east and at Chichester Harbour and Chichester gravel pits in the west. They suffer severely from predation by foxes, which take the eggs and the young, so active conservation is necessary, with electric fences and rafts moored in the gravel pits to provide safe nesting sites. By August the young are flying with their parents, from which they can be distinguished by their shorter tails and dark wings. The adults are still quite territorial about their nesting sites on the shingle, where they loudly display even when the young have left the nest.

Left: The beautiful scarlet Pheasant's-eye (*Adonis annua*), photographed here on a field margin near Seaford, is a rare annual of disturbed or cultivated soils on the chalk. In Sussex it is known from Brighton (where it flowered by the tennis courts in Preston Park in 1993) to Beachy Head, but the number of flowering plants fluctuates greatly year by year. Seed can last for many years in the soil and germinate when the ground is disturbed.

Above: The Dark-green Fritillary can be found throughout the month on the Downs and on bracken-covered slopes of the heaths. Large and richly coloured, it has a dark green underside to the rear wings, which are marked with silver patches. It is a strong flier, nearly always perching with closed wings, and if disturbed flies a long way before alighting again.

Left: Moon carrot (*Sesile libanotis*) is a very rare umbellifer and, like its tiny relative Small Hare's-ear, is known in Sussex only from the Beachy Head area and a couple of other sites in eastern England. Seen here growing with the very common Wild Carrot (*Daucus carota*), it is distinguished by its smooth, not rough, stems and by the big, rounded dome of pure white flowers.

Henbane (*Hyoscyamus niger*) has declined nationally through loss of coastal habitat to development, but still occurs in Sussex, mainly in the eastern coastal area. It is a tall, bushy plant with big, creamy trumpet-shaped flowers with a dark throat, the petals marked with a fine network of brownish-purple veins. It often appears after ground is disturbed. In 1976 – the drought year – I was asked to check a field near Halland for a farmer who wished to graze his cows on the only 'greenery' available. The field in question had a fine mixed crop of Henbane and Thorn-apple (*Datura stramonium*), both highly poisonous. However, they are both unpalatable, and grazing animals usually avoid them.

Round-leved Fluellen (*Kickxia spuria*) occurs right across Sussex, both on the chalk and on the Weald clay, on open slopes and also on the margins of cultivated fields. The leaves differ from those of Sharp-leaved Fluellen (*K. elatine*) in being rounded at the base, while the upper lip of the flower is purple rather than violet in colour. It is low-growing and easily missed, but very pretty.

Wall Germander (*Teucrium chamaedrys*) is a Red Data rare species, with seven known sites in Britain, of which that at Cuckmere Haven is the only one where it is considered to be a native plant. There it grows in very short turf, the pink flowers each bearing a large, showy lower lip.

Clustered Bellflower (*Campanula glomerata*) is a familiar flower of late summer on chalk grassland, where it is locally frequent.

Elecampane (*Inula helenium*) is a tall, elegant plant with big, broad leaves and flowers like small sunflowers. Introduced from the East, it exists in a few scattered sites in Sussex, usually in roadside hedgerows. It was used in the 18th and 19th centuries to treat horses with 'sore shins' – the result of a day's hard work pulling a stage coach. The big leaves are woolly underneath. They were soaked in a bucket of hot water and wrapped round the horse's leg as a poultice. Many of the sites where it still exists are therefore along the old coach roads or beside what was once a coaching inn.

Small and Essex Skippers (*left and right respectively*) are on the wing at the same time, from late July and throughout August, and are common in rough grassland, buzzing about like little bees. The Essex Skipper, pictured feeding on Viper's-bugloss, can be distinguished at close range by examining the tips of the antennae, which look like black full stops.

Second-brood Adonis Blues are flying at the same time as Chalkhill Blues on chalk down grassland. They are easily distinguished by colour, Adonis Blue (*left*) being a gorgeous kingfisher blue, while the Chalkhill Blue is a pale sky blue.

Meachants, Willingdon.

Right: Round-headed Rampion (*Phyteuma orbiculare*) goes by the common name of 'Pride of Sussex'. Here it is being visited by a Six-spot Burnet moth. It is common on the chalk downs of east Sussex, but less so on downland in the west.

Below: The first of the late-flowering helleborines, the Marsh Helleborine (*Epipactis palustris*) comes into bloom in August. In the past it occurred widely in marshes across Susssex and at the base of the north slopes of the Downs where springs emerged. It is now restricted to east Sussex, with a fading colony at Balcombe and a thriving one at Rye Harbour. When examined closely, it has some resemblance to the much-cultivated *Cymbidium* orchids, with a beautifully red-striped base of the lip, which terminates in a white-frilled epichile bearing a yellow, crinkly plate.

White-letter Hairstreak butterflies lay their eggs on Common Elm or Wych Elm, the former now much reduced by the ravages of Dutch Elm disease, and they love to feed on bramble blossom, as above. Small colonies still persist on Wych Elm, but it has become rare. The undersides of the wings are marked with a white 'W'.

Above: Clouded yellow butterflies appear in Sussex when they enjoy a particularly good breeding season in mainland Europe and spill over across the Channel. Unlike the spring-flying Brimstone, they are a rich golden-yellow with black wing edges. They especially like to feed on the flowers of Lucerne and clovers.

Below: Honeysuckle is a common flower in Sussex, but Fly Honeysuckle (*Lonicera xylosteum*) is very rare – and not a climber. It is to be found only in scrub on the north slope of the Downs near Amberley.

Marsh Gentian (*Gentiana pneumonanthe*) is the only truly blue gentian to flower in the autumn in Britain. Last seen in west Sussex in 1968 near Amberly, it is now only to be found in about 20 sites in east Sussex, mainly on Ashdown Forest.

Above: When you are looking for Marsh Gentians (*facing page*), keep a wary eye open for the Silver-studded Blue butterfly, which feeds on gorse, broom and heather. It is small, with a fluttering flight, settling with half-closed wings, which make it a little easier to spot.

Right: In late August we occasionally experience strong easterly winds, which can bring exotic visitors to Sussex across the North Sea. This young White Stork appeared at Itford in 1984 and took up residence on the roof of the farmhouse. White Storks are rare vagrants, but they are being seen with increasing frequency in east and south-east England.

In this picture of the Firle Scarp, taken from near Lullington Heath, some cornfields bordered by poppies are nearing harvest time.

Above: This adult swift was brought to me to treat, having flown into a window and stunned itself. It made a rapid recovery and was released a couple of hours later.

Right: The Hobby was not so fortunate, having flown into a barbed-wire fence near Southease, badly lacerating one wing. This healed well post-operatively, but by the time the bird could fly it was too late for it to migrate south to Africa. A kindly falconer housed it, releasing it the following spring when its fellows had returned to breed.

Above left: Five autumn-flowering species of helleborine of the genus *Epipactis* occur in Sussex. The most frequently found is the Broad-leaved Helleborine (*Epipactis helleborine*), which is widely distributed across the county in sandy and calcareous woodland, especially under beech trees where there is a fair amount of sunlight. The flowers are pollinated by Common Wasps (*Vespa germanica*), which become totally inebriated on the nectar obtained from the base of the lip, and can be seen to fall off the flower to the ground, lying there buzzing feebly.

Above right: Violet Helleborine (*Epipactis purpurata*) flowers about ten days later than the Broad-leaved species, with a similar woodland distribution although in much smaller numbers. It tolerates much deeper shade in the woods where it grows. The leaves are slimmer, sharply pointed and often violet-tinged, while the flowers are paler. A curious and attractive form, which has been found near East Grinstead and around Arundel, is achlorophyllous, which means that is has no chlorophyll: the entire plant is a luminous shade of pinkish-mauve and the flowers are white.

The Banded Demoiselle is a beautiful little dragonfly which is locally common by streams and in river valleys north of the Downs, particularly along the River Arun, and is extending its range in east Sussex. August is a good time to see it.

More than 85 species of blackberry have been described in Sussex, their identification being a job for the specialist. Among the first to come into fruit is the Dewberry (*Rubus caesius*), which flourishes in waste ground, especially along the tracks of abandoned railway lines, many of which are now public footpaths. It is a low-growing, soft-foliaged species, whose fruits when ripe have a beautiful blue bloom like that of a grape. The flavour is a little bit tart, and the juice is bright red. The berries are difficult to pick as they tend to disintegrate, but they are well worth the effort.

September

This can be one of the most delightful months of the year, often enjoying settled weather and plenty of sunshine. In the countryside the harvest is in full swing and everywhere trees and bushes are laden with ripening fruit, a welcome source of food for migrating birds. The summer song birds and hirundines are all leaving on their southern journey. Sudden adverse changes in the weather can result in spectacular 'falls' of these migrants, especially along the coast where headlands jut out towards France.

Early in the morning one may find trees and bushes packed with sheltering warblers and flycatchers, which depart as soon as the light and an improvement in the weather allow them to go safely on their way. On warm afternoons, when rising air currents create good 'lift', the sky is the place to look for migrating birds of prey – falcons, buzzards and harriers

Facing page: This picture, taken in 1965 near Firle, illustrates a feature of the harvest which has gone for ever – oats cut by a reaper and binder, the sheaves stooked in rows.

Right: Black Bryony (*Tamus communis*) is a strong climber, growing annually from large underground tubers to a height of more than 3m in hedgerows throughout the county. By the time the fruits are mature in September the heart-shaped leaves have usually shrivelled, exposing the tight clusters of bright red berries. These are highly poisonous, producing a burning sensation in the mouth, followed by vomiting, purgation and, in rare circumstances, death by paralysis of the respiratory muscles. The taste is so unpleasant that animals and children seldom eat enough for this to occur. By late winter the toxicity appears to lessen, and birds will eat the berries without ill effect.

tt

Above: Anyone who has had a picnic on the South Downs in the autumn will have encountered Carline Thistle (*Carlina vulgaris*), which is small but extremely prickly. It is biennial, and the immature plants without flowers are hard to spot until you sit on them. The straw yellow flowers are most attractive.

Left: Autumn Lady's-tresses (*Spiranthes spiralis*) is the last of our native orchids to flower, growing in short grass on chalky or basic soils, particularly on lawns, tennis courts and in cemeteries, where it can appear in thousands. The leaves overwinter, and by flowering time they have withered and disappeared, so that the flowering stem appears to grow straight out of the soil. The tightly wound spiral flower spoke may twist either left or right, each sweetly scented flower being rich in necar, attracting small flies, beetles and bumblebees. Numbers appear to fluctuate greatly year by year, but in fact many plants are there but not flowering – and of course showing no leaves to betray their presence.

Another sight which, like the stooks on page 92, has disappeared from the Sussex countryside. This photograph shows traditional round Sussex stacks being thatched at Plashett Park Farm, near Ringmer, in 1966.

Among the rare birds which can be blown off course from the continent to Sussex on its migration south is the Spoonbill. They are delightful to watch as they fish in ponds and lakes. They are appearing in Sussex much more frequently in recent years, and it is likely that before long they will return here as a breeding species. Birds which have bred not far away in the Netherlands are among the visitors.

One of the joys of autumn: a beech wood with fallen leaves glowing in the sun.

The Kestrel is our commonest bird of prey, frequently to be seen hunting in open country and farmland. Their ability to hover in mid-air as they scan the ground for small prey has earned them the name 'Windhover'. Here a female has just caught a large beetle.

Wheatears often stay around for days on the coast, as here at Pevensey, before resuming their journey south. They once earned a good income for farmers on the Downs, who would trap them and sell them to local hotels, where they appeared on the menu as ortolan.

At Sidlesham Ferry, towards the far west of the county – an RSPB reserve famous for attracting migrating waders – a Dunlin (*left*) and a Little Stint feed along the low-tide line.

Above: Blackberries (*Rubus fructicosus* agg.) are now at their best. The 85 species show enormous variety in size, in the shape of the fruits and, especially, in flavour. Blackberrying is one of the real pleasures of the autumn, and you don't have to be tall: as a small child I could always find splendid berries to pick below the level the grown-ups could reach.

Right: Wild Pear trees (*Pyrus pyraster*) are unusual plants of woods and hedges in both west and east Sussex. They probably derive from culitivated pears or their discarded fruits. The fruit is often more rounded in shape than expected, and in September is very hard and tasteless. The old Sussex name of Stone Pear is very apt.

Above: Deadly Nightshade (*Atropa belladonna*) can be locally frequent in scrub on the Downs and elsewhere in woods. The plants are perennial, up to 1.5m tall, and in September they carry large black fruits as big as cherries, set in a star-shaped calyx with five lobes. Deadly Nightshade has been cultivated since Roman times for its medicinal properties, but it is dangerous, too: animals rarely eat it, but it is attractive to children, and symptoms of poisoning can occur following the ingestion of a single berry.

Left: Elder (*Sambucus nigra*) is a very common shrub found in woodlands and hedgerows throughout the county. Unripe, or even undercooked, berries are toxic and can cause nausea and diarrhoea, with an accelerated heart rate. By September the berries are properly ripe, shining black and easily detached from the red stalks. Elderberries are widely used to make wine, jellies and preserves. They are also a great attraction to blackbirds, thrushes of all sorts and especially greenfinches, which end up with purple-stained heads – causing slight identification problems for bird watchers.

October

This is the time of year when we see the full glory of autumn coloration in the leaves of trees and bushes everywhere. Rose hips are abundant in the hedgerows. Dog Rose (*Rosa canina*) is widespread across Sussex, as is Field Rose (*R. arvensis*), whose distinctive hips are rounded, with the withered style projecting from the apex like a spent matchstick. Many other species of wild rose occur in Sussex, but they are not easy to indentify correctly.

One fascinating plant to be found on coastal shingles and sands, as at Camber, is Sea Buckthorn (*Hippophae rhamnoides*). It is not easy to pick the orange-coloured fruits, as the bushes are armed with vicious thorns, but they can be used to make a rather nice, tangy-flavoured jelly to serve with fish.

Dogwood (*Cornus sanguinea*) is a common hedgerow shrub, with black berries borne in a cluster on bright red stalks. In medieval times the fruits were used as a mild laxative. Chaucer mentions them as 'gaitrys beryis' in the Nun's Priest's Tale, where Pertelote, the hen, recommends them to her husband, Chauntecleer:

Above: Dogwood berries have a mild laxative effect.

Facing page: An October morning by the Bevern stream near Barcombe.

> *A day or two ye shul have digestyves*
> *Of worms, er ye take your laxatyves*
> *Of lawriol . . . or of gaitrys beryis . . .*
> *Pekke hem up right up as they growe and ete hem yn!*

October is not always 'the season of mists and mellow fruitfulness', but when the weather is fine the quality of light on a misty morning is special.

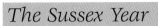

Of the two Dog Roses, *Rosa canina* is the more common. The hips are smooth and slightly elongated, borne on short stalks. By the time the hips are ripe, all traces of the petals and sepals have disappeared. Dog Rose is widespread in thickets and hedgerows.

Field Rose, *Rosa arvensis*, is the less common, occurring in hedges and woodland clearings. it is reasonably easy to identify, the rounded hips carried in erect, long-stalked clusters, each hip capped with a withered black style.

Sea Buckthorn (*Hippophaë rhamnoides*) at Camber Sands.

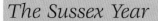

Above: The Great Gale of 1967 devastated woodland as well as buildings in Sussex, but surprisingly few grazing animals outside at the time suffered injury. One pair of horses on the clifftop at Peacehaven remained totally unscathed while their stable disappeared, never to be found. This picture shows cows grazing at the head of Malling Coombe in Lewes just after the storm.

Right: Wild Service-tree (*Sorbus torminalis*) grows across the northern half of Sussex. Confined to the clay soils, it is often found as a hedgerow plant, but occasionally as a fine standard tree up to 25m tall. The leaves turn a gorgeous yellow in autumn, while the fruits are brown, their surface decorated with russet-coloured scales. Later in the month they will ripen, becoming soft and dark brown, a process known as 'bletting', which renders them edible, with a flavour similar to that of prunes. The name is derived from the Latin for beer, *cerevisia*, as the Romans used the fruit of the related True Service-tree (*S. domestica*) as a flavouring. As late as the 19th century the fruits were sold as 'chequers' in markets, and the name became popular for public houses, which often had a Chequer tree nearby.

An October view of Lewes from Offham chalkpit.

Looking east along the Downs from Blackcap, near Plumpton, on a fine October day.

Above: Many summer migrant birds have already left us by October, but a few linger on, such as this Osprey at Barcombe reservoir. These are often young birds, and they may stay for some days, fishing on reservoirs or lakes before departing for their winter quarters in Africa.

Above left: Purple Sandpipers breed far to the north of Sussex, but winter along the coast in small groups. They may be found feeding among seaweed-covered rocks at Pett Level, Eastbourne, Littlehampton near the mouth of the River Arun and in a number of sites west to Pagham Harbour.

Left: Kittiwakes now breed in good numbers on the cliffs at Splash Point, Seaford. In winter some roost at high tide with the Purple Sandpipers on the piers at either side of Newhaven Harbour, where these photographs were taken.

A late October day to the west of Ditchling Beacon, where ploughing of the chalky flint soil has created striking patterns.

Left: Many fruiting bushes produce ripe fruit in late October, among them Juniper (*Juniperus communis*), with its spiky foliage and purple-black fruits which take two years to ripen. Sadly this species is disappearing from its downland haunts and can be found only in west Sussex.

Centre: Yew (*Taxus baccata*) is widely distributed across Sussex, especially on chalky and basic soils, with a fine stand at the Kingley Vale reserve in west Sussex. All parts of the plant are highly toxic, except for the pink, fleshy aril which surrounds the seed. This is eaten by a wide variety of birds, the poisonous seed passing undigested through the intestinal tract. Sheep and cattle will eat yew, especially if it has been cut from a tree or hedge, and heart failure rapidly ensues. Horses and pigs are very sensitive to yew poisoning, but there is some evidence that deer can develop a tolerance, browsing it with apparent impunity.

Right: One of the more unusual October fruiters is Duke of Argyll's Tea-plant (*Lycium barbarum*), which flourishes near the coast, as at Tide Mills, near Newhaven. It was introduced to Britain from China in 1696, the common name deriving from a nurseryman's mistake when supplying the then Duke of Argyll, who had ordered tea plants.

The Firecrest is a late autumn migrant. These tiny birds may be found in sheltered bushes and copses, especially near the coast. They are distinguished from their close relative, the Goldcrest, by their prominent black and white eyestripes.

A recent addition from Europe to the fauna of Sussex, the Wasp Spider (*Argiope bruennichi*) is now well established along coastal Sussex and has spread inland. It is a large spider, the black and yellow banded abdomen giving it its common name. Look for it in your garden!

Sloes are the fruit of Blackthorn (*Prunus spinosa*), the blossom of which is such a feature of the hedges in March. (*See page 18.*) Sloes are small plums, blue-black in colour with an attractive bloom on the skin when ripe. The flesh is green, with a very sharp taste that dries the mouth. Sloes are widely gathered to make sloe gin, the spirit extracting the flavour, judiciously sweetened with sugar. They also make an excellent jelly.

A prostrate form of the Blackthorn also grows on shingle near the sea. In certain years it fruits so abundantly that the bushes are entirely hidden by a mound of sloes.

Spindle (*Euonymus europaeus*) is fairly common on chalky soils, especially beside streams and ditches. It is often unnoticed until the fruits ripen, abundantly in some years. They are a brilliant pink colour, with four lobes which split to reveal bright orange seeds. It is poisonous, causing severe gastric disturbance, mental confusion and loss of consciousness. Poisoning of animals is not uncommon, and also of children who are attracted by the pretty fruits. In the past the close-textured wood of mature trees was used for the manufacture of spindles used in weaving.

Guelder-rose (*Viburnum opulus*) grows in woods and hedgerows on moist clay soils, being widespread and common across the northern part of both west and east Sussex. The palmate leaves turn a beautiful red in October, but their colour is nothing compared with that of the clusters of glowing red fruits. These should not be eaten, as they are slightly toxic.

November

The month is renowned for unpleasant weather – rain, gales and early dark evenings. The flowers have all finished, the summer bird visitors have long since gone, and yet there is still plenty of interest to see. Wintering geese and ducks are beginning to appear, the flocks building up steadily during the month as cold weather in Scandinavia and eastern Europe pushes the birds towards our milder shores.

The same weather patterns force the winter thrushes, Redwings and Fieldfares, across the North Sea, often in large numbers, to take advantage of the feast of Hawthorn and Rowan berries not already stripped by other hungry beaks.

On the stubble fields and pastures the wintering flocks of native-bred Lapwings are complemented by others from further afield, sometimes joined by smartly plumaged Golden Plovers, a few still sporting the black bellies of their summer breeding finery.

Right: Large flocks of Brent Geese are one of the attractions of Pagham and Chichester Harbours in winter.

Facing page: This is the time of year to get out into the marshes, especially in west Sussex, as here on Thorney Island. The onset of cold weather brings wintering wildfowl and waders in huge flocks to feed on the mudflats exposed at low tide.

Autumn tints reflected in the still
waters of the Ouse, north of Lewes.

Above: The berries of the Rowan (*Sorbus aucuparia*) are a valuable source of food for birds in the winter months.

Right: November usually sees the first frosts of the winter, here bejewelling a large spider's web. It can be a revelation to realise just how many spiders there are in the grass when we find their webs covered with dewdrops or frost in the early morning.

Canada Geese are well established all over Sussex as breeding birds. They are not always welcome, because their aggressive behaviour drives away nesting native water birds. In winter they congregate in large flocks in the river valleys and arable fields, often flying in to reservoirs to roost at night.

Surprising things happen, even in November. Here a Glow-worm larva sits on a Dwarf Thistle flower on the top of Malling Down on a mild November day.

December

The days may be short, but December is a month with a fair amount of fine weather to encourage us out into the country, to walk and perhaps to work off the effects of seasonal celebrations. This is the time to make sure that our garden birds are well supplied with food and, no less important, with water. They will amply repay us with their colour and activities.

Among the usual visiting tits and finches, look out for Siskins (small green finches, the males with black foreheads) and Bramblings (similar in size and colour to Chaffinches, but with a dark head and a prominent white rump, which shows in flight.)

The woodlands may be devoid of bird song, but on the marshes and along the coast the wintering birds are a great attraction, with exotic northerners such as Goldeneye, Smew, Goosander and Red-throated Diver to look for.

Facing page: Near Cooksbridge, after a light snowfall, the blue Downs are just visible against an evening sunset.

Right: Those of us old enough to remember the days before central heating became the norm will remember the 'frost flowers' on the inside of the bathroom window on very cold winter days. The move from the warmth of the bath to the icy bedroom needed to be made with rapidity!

Snowy scene with sheep near Laughton.

Less numerous than Teal or Wigeon, the larger Pintail is an elegant duck, with very long central tail feathers – clear to see at rest or in flight. The drakes have dark heads which contrast beautifully with their long white necks. They are usually silent, although the drake has a low whistling call.

Heavy snowfall is a real trial for birds such as the Common Snipe, pictured here, since they are unable to probe with their long beaks into the frozen ground to feed.

Above: Cattle Egret at Selhurst Park, in west Sussex. These are chunky little herons with pale orange legs and chestnut-crowned heads. They stand with hunched shoulders, which gives them a rather dejected appearance. Abroad, they congregate with cattle in the fields, foraging for insects attracted by the warmth of their bodies, and even standing on them to pick off parasites such as ticks – a task executed with great delicacy. Over the next few years we may well expect them to breed in Sussex.

The closely related Little Egret is completely white, with dark legs and bright yellow feet which are clear to see when they are flying. They now breed regularly in both east and west Sussex in small numbers.

Right: December sees big invasions of wintering ducks on reservoirs, lakes and wetlands. Common Teal are small ducks, the drakes having chestnut and green heads, beautifully barred flanks, a white wing flash and a yellow rump. Their call is a musical trill.

Above: Wigeon gather in large flocks on the coastal grasslands where they graze. In flight the drakes have a prominent white wing panel, while in close-up you can see that the chestnut coloured head is crowned with a creamy gold forehead. Their high whistling call is a familar sound to anyone walking the marshes in winter.

Holly (*Ilex aquifolia*) is inseparable from December and Christmas time, when its dark foliage and red berries are an important and traditional part of the festive decorations. Equally important is the value of Holly berries as a food for hungry birds in the cold days of winter. Many species enjoy them, and flocks of thrushes and pigeons can quickly strip a tree of every berry. Holly trees with what appear to be ripe fruits are sometimes inexplicably ignored by the birds, who may return much later in winter to eat them. Occasionally you may see a particularly aggressive Mistle Thrush commandeer a Holly tree and drive off all competitors.

Ivy (*Hedera helix*) also ripens in December, the berries providing a very useful dietary addition for birds, especially blackbirds and wood pigeons. It is widespread across Sussex in woods and hedgerows, and also on cliffs, climbing up to 30m. There are several exotic ivy species with which it can easily be confused. The berries are poisonous to man, and contact with the foliage can produce dermatitis. Cattle will eat ivy, resulting in tainted milk, and if large quantities are consumed they will stagger about, bellowing loudly and showing obvious signs of hyperaesthesia – excessive sensitivity.

Above: Mistletoe (*Viscum album*) is the other traditional Christmas berry. Found in scattered sites across Sussex, it is parasitic on broad-leaf trees, especially apple, poplar and plum. The berries are much enjoyed by birds, especially Mistle Thrushes – hence the name. The pulp is very sticky, causing the birds to wipe their beaks on the tree bark, thereby spreading the seeds. Mistletoe is poisonous, consumption of 3–4 berries by a child or ten by an adult producing symptoms of nausea, vomiting and diarrhoea.

Right: Butcher's-broom (*Ruseus aculeatus*) is an interesting shrub, most often found in dry oak woods and hedgerows. The fat red berries appear to be carried in the middle of the leaves, but these are not real leaves but modified stems called cladodes. The minute star-shaped male and female flowers, produced at the same time, sit in the middle of them. The berries were widely used medicinally in the Middle Ages, while the green branches were tied together and formed into brooms used by butchers for cleaning their chopping blocks.

The tradition of snow at Christmas is not always realised in these days of warmer winters, but here at Southease Church the congregation at a carol concert had problems driving back up the steep hill to the main road after the service.